D1784230

SUN & MOON SIGNS

LEO

James Petulengro

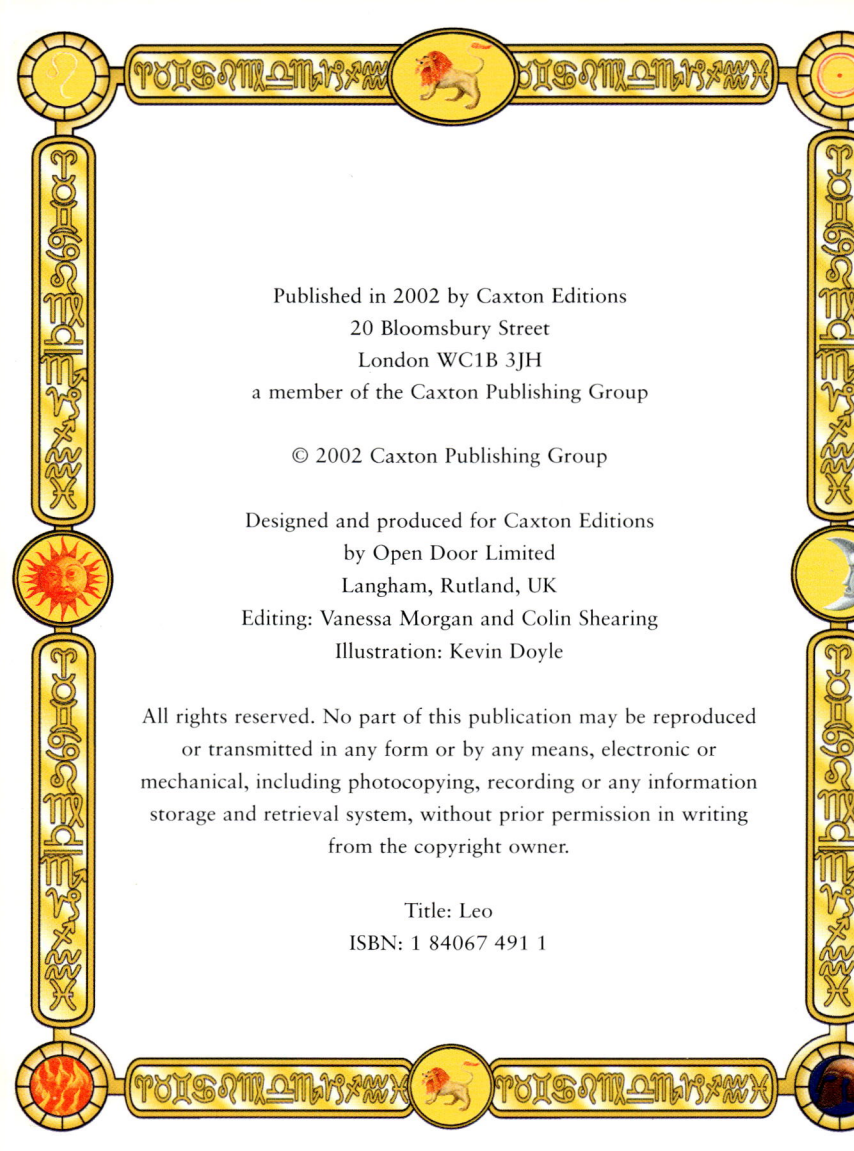

Published in 2002 by Caxton Editions
20 Bloomsbury Street
London WC1B 3JH
a member of the Caxton Publishing Group

© 2002 Caxton Publishing Group

Designed and produced for Caxton Editions
by Open Door Limited
Langham, Rutland, UK
Editing: Vanessa Morgan and Colin Shearing
Illustration: Kevin Doyle

All rights reserved. No part of this publication may be reproduced
or transmitted in any form or by any means, electronic or
mechanical, including photocopying, recording or any information
storage and retrieval system, without prior permission in writing
from the copyright owner.

Title: Leo
ISBN: 1 84067 491 1

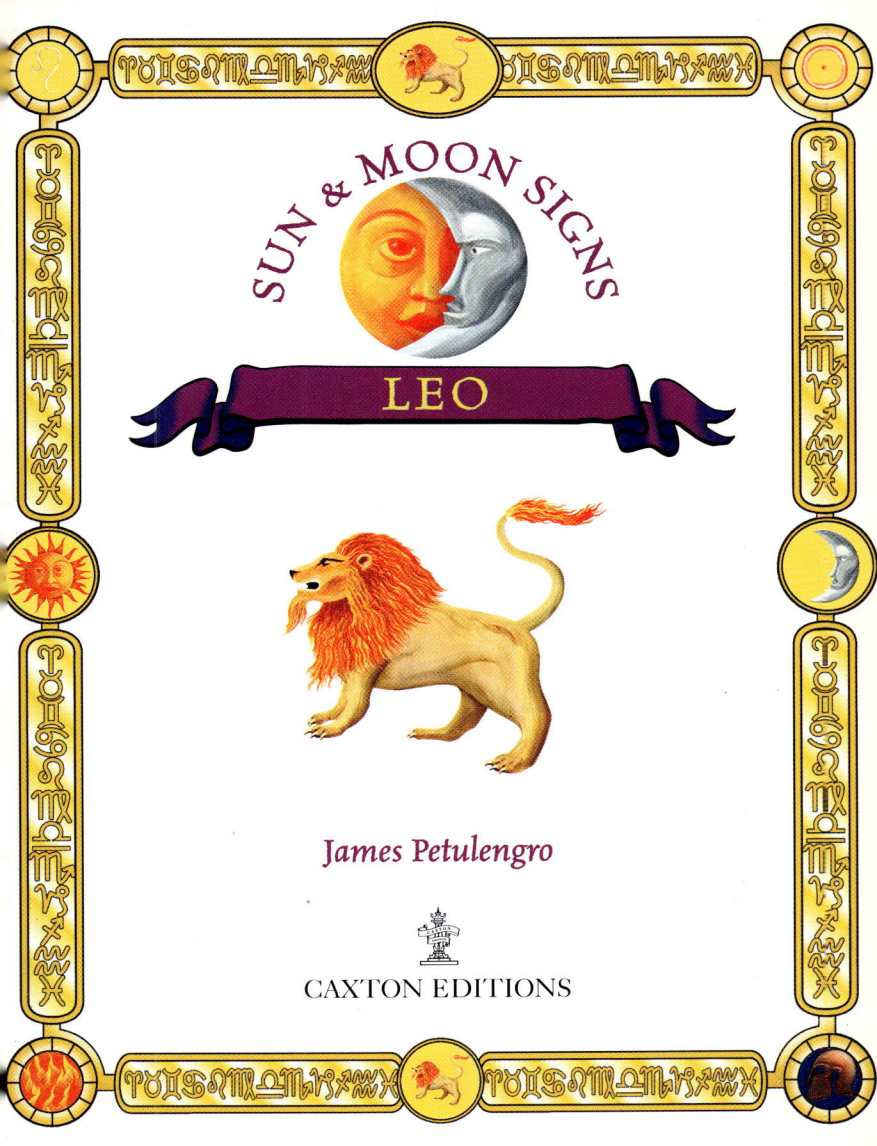

SUN & MOON SIGNS

LEO

James Petulengro

CAXTON EDITIONS

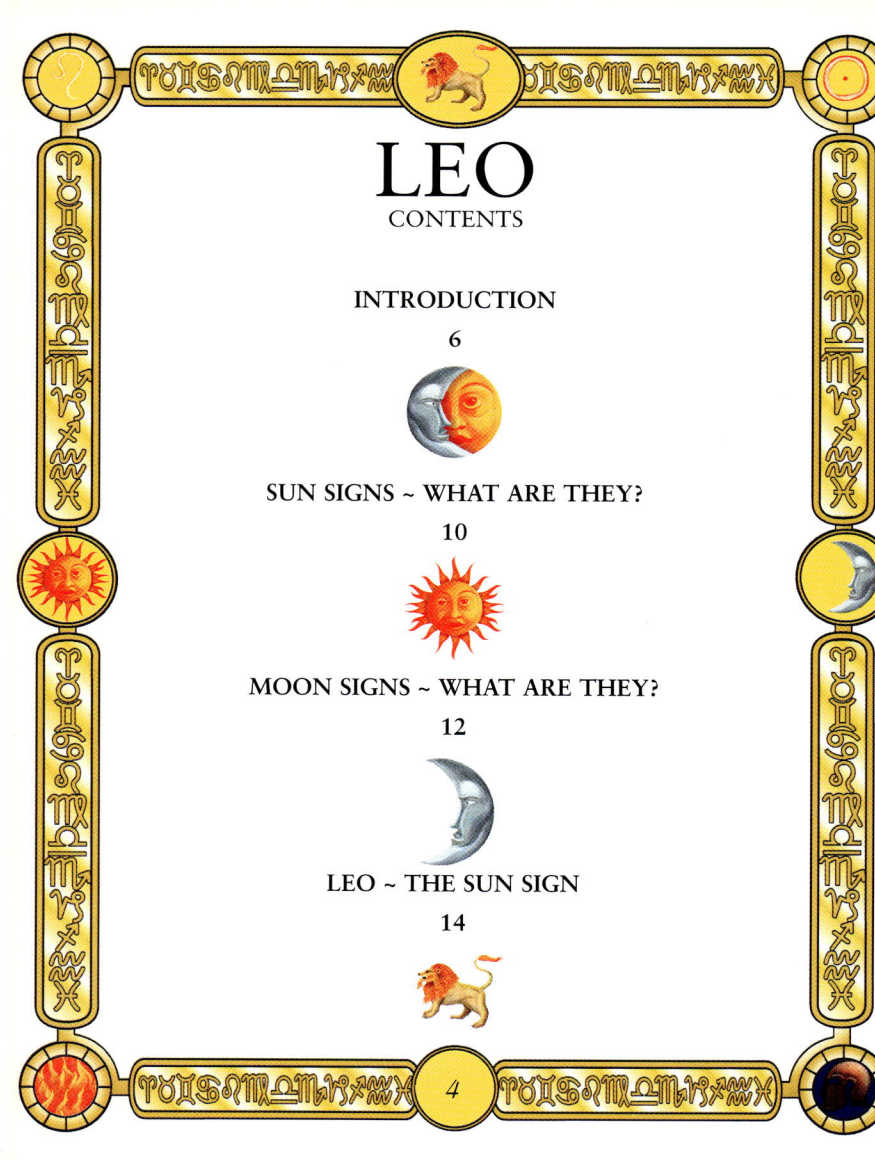

LEO
CONTENTS

LEO

CONTENTS

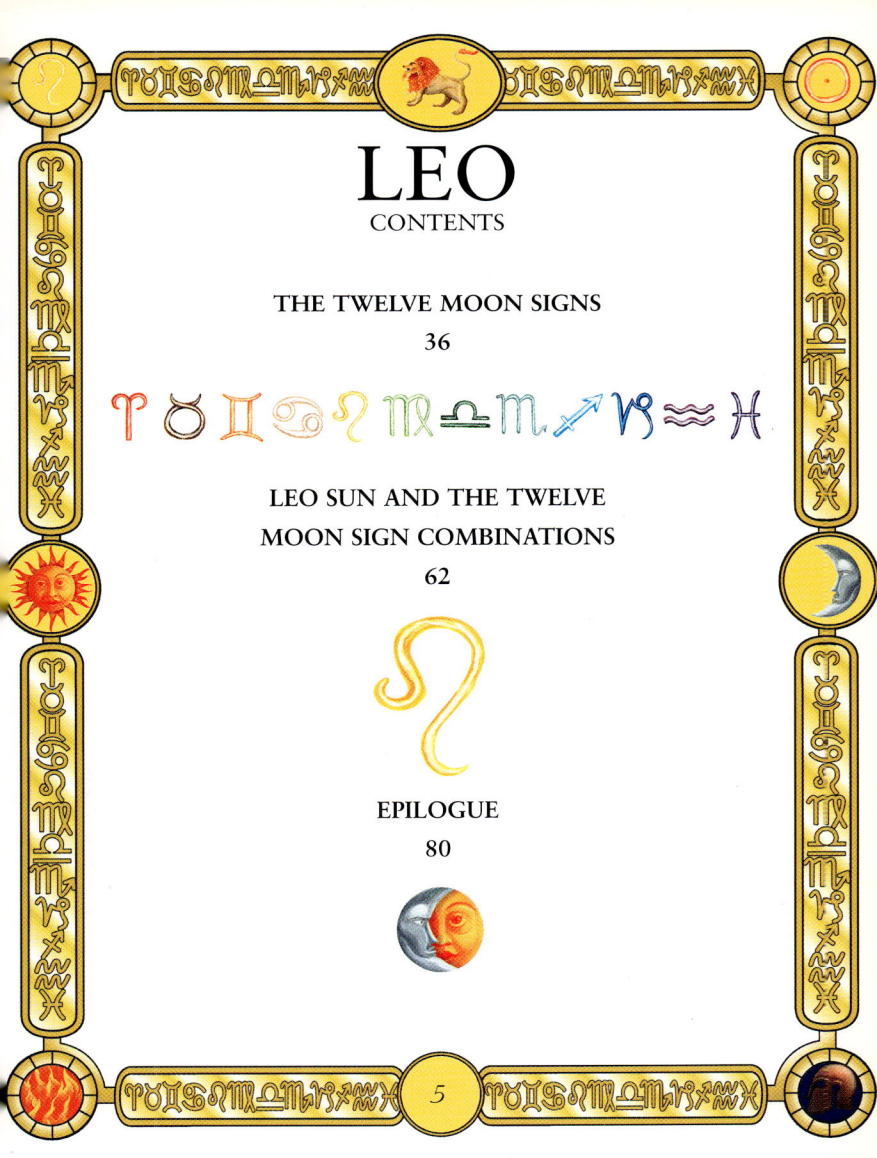

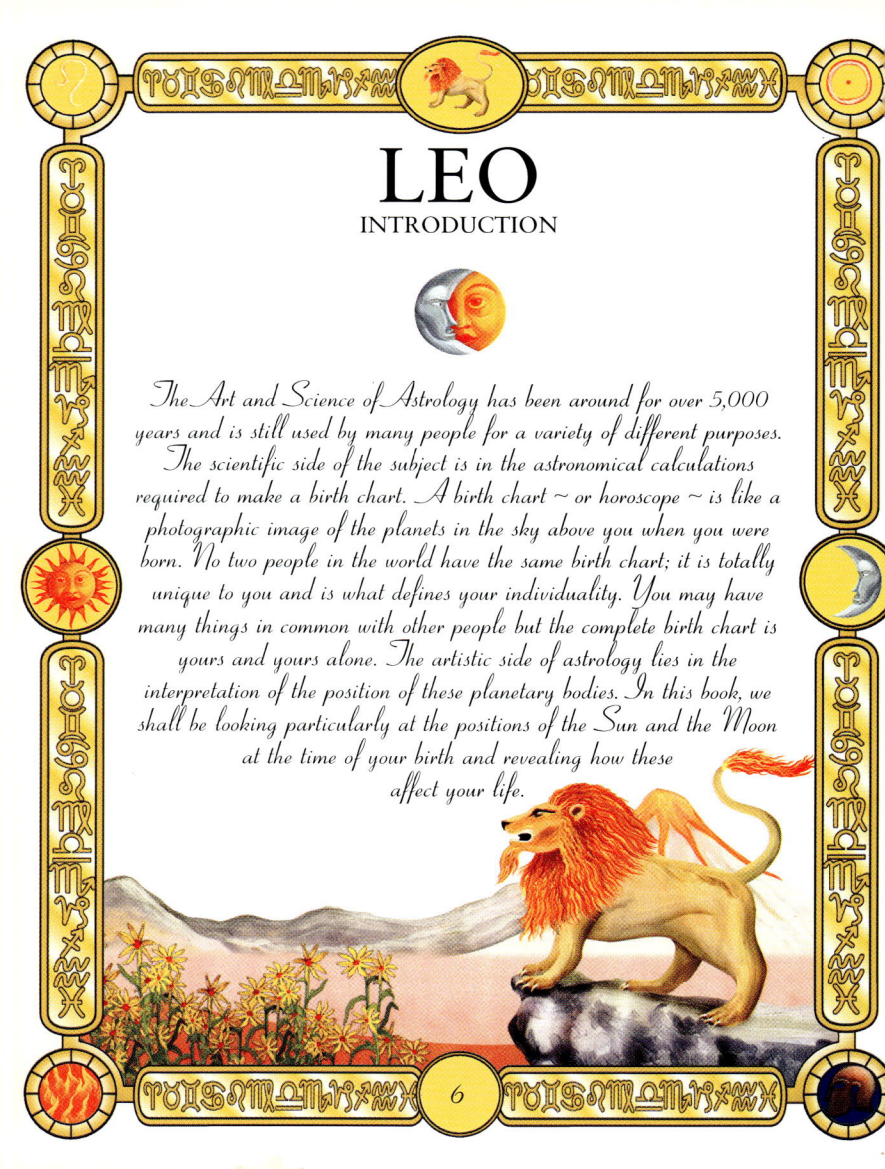

LEO

INTRODUCTION

The Art and Science of Astrology has been around for over 5,000 years and is still used by many people for a variety of different purposes. The scientific side of the subject is in the astronomical calculations required to make a birth chart. A birth chart ~ or horoscope ~ is like a photographic image of the planets in the sky above you when you were born. No two people in the world have the same birth chart; it is totally unique to you and is what defines your individuality. You may have many things in common with other people but the complete birth chart is yours and yours alone. The artistic side of astrology lies in the interpretation of the position of these planetary bodies. In this book, we shall be looking particularly at the positions of the Sun and the Moon at the time of your birth and revealing how these affect your life.

Introduction

You may find that if you were born from the 19th to the 23rd of the month your Sun sign is what is called "on the cusp". Each year the Sun enters the various Sun signs on different days so just because you were born on the 21st of the month, for example, does not necessarily mean you are the Sun sign you think you are. Calculating your birth chart will help you to discover exactly what your Sun sign is.

As a special feature, if you do not have one already, you can calculate your own birth chart including a short 8-page interpretation on my website at http://www.jamespetulengro.co.uk type in your birth details and you can then print out astrological details and your birth chart. This may also help you when you come to look at the Moon sign part of this book and the Sun and Moon combinations if you do not know your Moon sign.

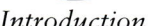

Introduction

The 12 Zodiac signs are traditionally formed into four groups, within which they interact and complement each other.

First come the four elements. These consist of Fire signs, Earth signs, Air signs and Water signs. The Fire signs are, by nature, enthusiastic and they consist of Aries, Leo and Sagittarius. The Earth signs are Taurus, Virgo and Capricorn and they are practical. The Air signs of Gemini, Libra and Aquarius are intellectual, while the Water signs of Cancer, Scorpio and Pisces are emotional.

A second group is known as the qualities. The cardinal signs are Aries, Cancer, Libra and Capricorn and they tend to be outgoing. The fixed signs of Taurus, Leo, Scorpio and Aquarius tend to be rigid in their opinions. The mutable signs of Gemini, Virgo, Sagittarius and Pisces are flexible and adaptable.

Introduction

The third group is positivity/masculinity and negativity/femininity. The positive signs are Aries, Gemini, Leo, Libra, Sagittarius and Aquarius. These people tend to be extroverts. The negative/feminine signs are Taurus, Cancer, Virgo, Scorpio, Capricorn and Pisces and these signs make people introvert. Do not be confused if you are a Leo woman as this does not mean that you lack femininity any more than a man with a feminine Sun sign lacks masculinity, although Leo is regarded as one of the male signs.

The fourth and last group is known as the polarities. This shows the special relationship a sign has with its polar opposite. Polar signs complement each other so that there is a special rapport and depth of understanding between them. For example, as Leo is one of the most royal of signs, Aquarius, its polar opposite, is the Zodiac sign of the people. Ruling planets: each sign is ruled by one of the planets and each planet has a very similar energy to the sign it rules. For example, Leo is ruled by the god Apollo, who brings light into our world as he races his golden chariot across the sky.

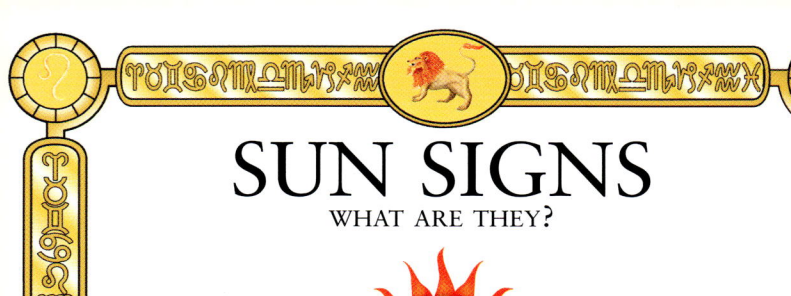

SUN SIGNS

WHAT ARE THEY?

The Sun is the star at the centre of our solar system, which is composed of nine planets. The Earth is the third in, at a distance of 93 million miles. The Sun is 109 times the size of Earth and, without it, there would be no life. It is the most powerful of all the bodies in our solar system and exerts a gravitational pull upon all of us. It affects each of our personalities so strongly that a very accurate picture can be given to the person who is born under each particular sign and it will continue to stamp that person with those characteristics throughout their life. The Sun is the fuel of our solar system, just as the Sun is the fuel of your personality.

Your Sun sign or sign of the Zodiac depends on the month of the year in which you were born because the Earth travels around the Sun once in approximately 365 days and the Sun appears to travel through one of twelve constellations in the sky above. Looking at your

Sun Signs – What are They?

Sun sign should not be confused with studying the daily horoscopes that you will find in many magazines or newspapers. In this book we are examining the effect that your Sun sign has on your personality, rather than predictions. You were born between 21st July and 21st August, which makes you a Leo.

Some astrologers feel that the Sun sign is too much of a generalisation, like believing that all butchers, bakers and candlestick makers are the same. However, the Sun, as I said earlier, is the most powerful body in our whole life and that reflects in the accuracy of Sun sign readings. If you know someone's Sun sign, then you are certainly much better informed about that person than you would otherwise be.

Your Sun sign personality is the personality that you enjoy flaunting and showing off to people because it is what you cherish. It is also what you are most proud of about yourself. To be more specific, the placement of your Sun generally represents how you express your ego. In many senses, a person's Sun sign will indicate how they present themselves to the world during daylight hours, while their Moon sign will indicate how they present themselves as dusk arrives and their more intimate, emotional side comes out.

MOON SIGNS

WHAT ARE THEY?

The Moon is the Earth's satellite and is approximately 250,000 miles away. Although only small in diameter ~ just 2,160 miles ~ the Moon exerts considerable gravitational influence on the Earth and is responsible for the tides. It orbits the Earth in approximately 28 days, known as the lunar cycle, and passes through each sign of the Zodiac every 2.5 days. In your birth chart it is considered almost as important as the Sun, but its influences are different. The Moon holds sway over your moods and emotional life. Whereas the Sun is your day, the Moon represents the night.

Your Moon sign represents how you deal with and express your tender, caring emotions and your emotional responses in general. It represents your instinctive, unconscious, primitive, habitual personality and much of your relationship to your emotions and expression

Moon Signs – What are They?

is affected by your Moon sign. It represents your basic emotional needs and how you feel most secure interacting with others. It represents your gut instinct and how you react to things when you are caught by surprise, particularly when you feel you are threatened. Another important area that the Moon controls is that of your domestic arena. Due to it being the planet that rules Cancer, the Moon is seen as feminine, watery, negative and reflective.

Some people do have both the same sign for the Sun and the Moon, ruling both their ego and emotions in the same way. This will generally provide a clear, personal consistency through many situations in your life.

Above: your Moon sign represents how you deal with and express your tender, caring emotions

LEO
THE SUN SIGN

If you are a Leo, and if we met and I began to explain to you your personality through your horoscope, you would love every minute of it because it would make you the centre of attention. Leos love to hear about themselves more than anything else.

Leo

21st July to 21st August

Positive Traits

Proud, dynamic, noble, loyal, sunny, happy-go-lucky, brave, warm-hearted, courageous, loving, faithful, generous

Negative Traits

Bossy, egotistical, vain, carefree, self-centred, haughty, pompous, interfering, over-dramatic

Traditional Associations

Zodiac Symbol: *The Lion*
Glyph: *♌*
Ruling Planet: *The Sun*
Ruling House: *The Fifth*
Gender: *Masculine and Positive*
Polarity: *Aquarius*
Element: *Fire*
Quality: *Fixed*
Key Phrase: *I create*
Body Area: *The heart and solar plexus, spine and back*
Colour: *Yellow*
Metal: *Gold*
Gemstone: *Tiger's eye and peridot*
Foods: *Peppermint, rosemary, rue, saffron, rice, honey, vine fruits*
Flora: *Sunflower, marigold, passion-flower, laurel, olive, palm, citrus*
Countries: *Lebanon, South of France, Romania, Sicily, Italy*
Cities: *Portsmouth, Bath, Prague, Rome, Bombay, Los Angeles, Madrid*
Tarot Card: *Strength*
Deities: *Apollo and Helios*
Activity: *Pleasure*

Leo – the Sun Sign

Leo is fiery and ruled by the Earth's star, the Sun. Since this Sun sign is ruled by the Sun itself, this bestows the strongest personality or ego of all the Zodiac. As a fixed sign, Leos are dogmatic in their opinions. This is also the most noble of all the signs.

As the fifth sign, Leo represents high summer, creativity and pleasure. It is represented by the Lion and, accordingly, as King of the Jungle, Leo is the most regal of the signs. Like the Sun which illuminates the lives of all people through the day, Leos are blessed with a very cheerful and sunny disposition. They enjoy spreading this happiness throughout their world.

Above: like the Sun which illuminates the lives of all people through the day, Leos are blessed with a very cheerful and sunny disposition.

Leo – the Sun Sign

Just as the Sun is at the centre of our solar system, Leos believe themselves to be the centre of their universe and as such they feel indispensable to the world at large. Lions hate the dark and they are easily bored; they go through life seeking warmth, light-heartedness and fun whenever and wherever possible. Leos can be found in all the best places in town, enjoying themselves and the Leos who are not out and about will be living it up at home. There are no introverted Lions but there are Lions who act as if they are introverts – and that is important to remember; they are great actors. It is important that they are on centre stage, under the spotlights, whether they are on a real stage in a theatre, or on the stage of life. Everything for them is an Oscar-winning performance; they will even make a drama out of the simplest things in life, such as going shopping, carefully choosing what clothes to wear, having the right accessories with which to make a dramatic entrance, even at the local supermarket. Although they do have the capacity to make fun of their own foibles, no one else should ever make fun of Leos.

Leo, the King of the Jungle, rules all the other animals and that includes their friends and family. They hate to take orders and if anyone shows a lack of respect for their nobility they will roar.

Leo – the Sun Sign

Some Leos mellow with old age but they never lower their proud heads. Although they are very good at telling others how to manage their affairs, they are actually not so good at managing their own. They are loveable and have a real honesty incongruously mixed up with a transparent and vulnerable ego. Those born under Leo are easily wounded if they feel that their wisdom and generosity is not respected. However, they are most susceptible to flattery and the way to win an argument with a Leo is to tell them – in the middle of it – how wonderful they look.

Above: Leos can be found in all the best places in town, enjoying themselves and the Leos who are not out and about will be living it up at home.

Leo – the Sun Sign

Lions just cannot help feeling superior or behaving dramatically but they are extremely astute in their mental reasonings. They dislike wasting energy and they are the master of the commanding word, even though their sentences will always be slightly theatrical, sometimes more than slightly.

Leos express themselves generously and openly and often give almost embarrassingly extravagant compliments. They are not bashful about their displeasure either. Whatever they say, they mean. Their words may calm or inflame but they never fail to leave an impression. Their royal ways are at their best when they are acting as host or hostess. They have the ability to make everyone feel as if they are being entertained in a royal palace, always ensuring that everyone knows their place within the Lion's court.

The Lion is almost continually in the throes of passion, not just with their partners, but with life in general. They cannot live without love, even the shy pussycats, and without romance in their lives, it is as if their Sun has been eclipsed. Leos hate to be dependent on other people because of their pride but they need others to be dependent upon them. They are particularly kind and considerate towards the weak and helpless, although

they may occasionally roar that there is too much responsibility being put upon them. They pout and sulk in a very dramatic fashion but it never lasts long as they soon revert to their normal happy selves. They have a good sense of humour and enjoy a good laugh, although if it is at their own expense they will always do so with dignity.

Above: Leos express themselves generously and openly and often give almost embarrassingly extravagant compliments.

Leo – the Sun Sign

At heart, the typical Lion is a spectacular gambler, wildly extravagant, and wanting first-class and luxury all the way. They spend freely on fun and pleasure – sometimes too freely. They are very generous and if asked for a loan when they are short of cash they will even go out and borrow it from someone else before admitting that the King is not in a position to help his needy subjects. They do, however, accumulate wealth so that they can distribute to others, once they have provided themselves with all the luxury that these royal felines require. When they work, they work hard and when they play, they play hard. They also enjoy lounging around and are quite contented to be waited on, hand and foot.

Above: at heart, the typical Lion is a spectacular gambler, wildly extravagant, and wanting first-class and luxury all the way.

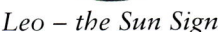

Leo – the Sun Sign

They enjoy gossip and feel hurt or left out if something is going on around them that they are not part of. The Lion may not have wanted to attend – preferring instead to laze about at home – but not to invite the King of the Jungle is a serious affront to their pride and feeling of status. The Lion alternates between being energetically gregarious and beautifully indolent. If they are involved in anything they usually ensure, through their flamboyant personality, that they are at the very heart of it. Because of their fixed nature they are difficult to sway from their set path and it is prudent for all to bow before these Kings or Queens of the Jungle.

The courage of the Lion is legendary. Even in *The Wizard of Oz,* the Cowardly Lion found that he had had courage all along. In the film *The Lion King,* the hero again overcame great adversity and protected all the other animals from their enemies. The world of film itself is always attractive to Leos, whether directing them, starring in them or just watching them and projecting themselves into the hero's role. In life, Leo needs to be a heroic figure and he will strive with great vigour and energy to attain that position.

Leo – the Sun Sign

YOUR BODY

The first thing to notice about a Leo is his mane. It is usually wavy, thick and worn in a wild and carefree style and it is their crowning glory. Their complexion is usually of a ruddy hue and they become flushed very easily. Some Leos seem to blush easily but often this blush is more a flush of pride or ego. Often their faces are pink because they have been exerting themselves too hard, or the love of their life is on their arm and they are proud to have them there.

Many Leos have dark brown eyes that seem soft and gentle at first – until they snap and crackle with fire. They have a commanding air and stately

bearing, as if they are looking down on all the other mortals beneath them. Their movements and speech are careful and deliberate. They seldom talk, run or even walk fast. The Lion is always centre stage in a crowd and makes dramatic movements with his body to emphasise a point. Leos also love to dress up in flamboyant and extravagant clothes that enhance and project their appearance of nobility. It is difficult to miss their vanity as they always seem to be looking at their own reflection, either in mirrors or any other reflective surface at hand.

Leo – the Sun Sign

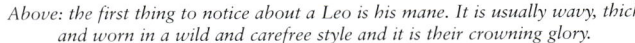

Above: the first thing to notice about a Leo is his mane. It is usually wavy, thick and worn in a wild and carefree style and it is their crowning glory.

Leo – the Sun Sign

YOUR POSSESSIONS

Leos are possessive and jealous. Whatever they own, whether a person or a thing, belongs to them mind, body and soul. Unlike the Taurus who actually needs to own, the Leo needs to love and 'to have, is to love'. Anything a Lion owns will be well looked after and fiercely protected.

They love surrounding themselves with luxurious, expensive items which they fill their palaces with. They are very attracted to gold, not just for its monetary value but for its aesthetic beauty. Leos are extremely astute and will not waste any time trying to 'get water out of a dry well'.

HOW YOU COMMUNICATE

Leos communicate as if they are trying to win an Oscar. They over-dramatise even the smallest situation. To them, life is large and they make their mark on it as rulers by letting everyone around them know who they are and what they believe in. They have strong and unshakeable opinions about everything. It is not wise to argue with a Leo, no matter how wrong they are, as they will not be moved by argument. Instead, they need flattering and to be told how wonderful they are and then the roaring Lion will turn into a gentle, purring pussycat.

Leo – the Sun Sign

Lions are also renowned for being bossy and often sound as if they are giving orders – which they usually are.

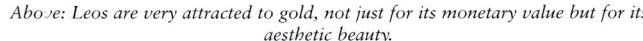

Above: Leos are very attracted to gold, not just for its monetary value but for its aesthetic beauty.

Leo – the Sun Sign

YOUR HOME LIFE

Leos make their homes as luxurious as they possibly can. The interior design will usually be flamboyant and dramatic with golden handles and rich velvet drapes. They love light and warmth, especially open fires which they can curl up in front of. Lions also like to live in warm climates if they can. Soft, comfortable furniture with plenty of cushions scattered around allow them to laze about in style. Again, mirrors will be abundant on account of the Lion's vanity. They love to entertain in their homes, often putting on extravagant parties for their many friends even if they cannot afford it.

Above: Leos prefer soft, comfortable furniture with plenty of cushions scattered around allow them to laze about in style.

Leo – the Sun Sign

YOUR CREATIVITY

Leos are extremely creative people and demonstrate this through artistic endeavours, particularly acting, whether professionally or as amateurs. They are drawn to all art that is bright and larger than life.

Lions rarely raise large families but make warm parents and have a great love for children, making them the perfect godparents. Lions are extremely kind and gentle with children.

Their own children will be lavished with affection and any discipline will be given with a firm roar but a gentle paw. They are also prone to giving their children long lectures as they have very strong, rigid beliefs on how children should behave. A child with a Leo parent swiftly learns to flatter their parent into submission. Leos can often be jealous of their children if they are getting more attention from their partners than themselves.

Above: Lions rarely raise large families but make warm parents and have a great love for children.

Leo – the Sun Sign

YOUR HEALTH

Leos are prone to high fevers, accidents and sudden illnesses but rarely suffer from chronic or lingering diseases. Leos seldom do anything by halves so they will either radiate incredible vitality or, if in minor discomfort, they will make as much noise about it as possible. 'Hear me roar' is what he says as he goes into dramatic death throes over a simple cold or a mild headache. They are not hypochondriacs but the sheer drama involved in being sick is just too much for them to pass up. A Lion who is seriously ill, however, will be too proud to say so. Either way, once they realise that they look weak, their pride will take over and they will be back on their feet, regardless of whether they are really better or not. A good indication of a sick Leo is if their mane looks unkempt and dull.

Leos may suffer from tension in the back or shoulders because sometimes they feel as though they are carrying the whole world upon their shoulders, as real kings do. Their heart, being the part of body ruled by the Sun is usually very strong, unless they are feeling unloved or suffering from a broken heart, in which case their heart will give them real physical problems.

Leo – the Sun Sign

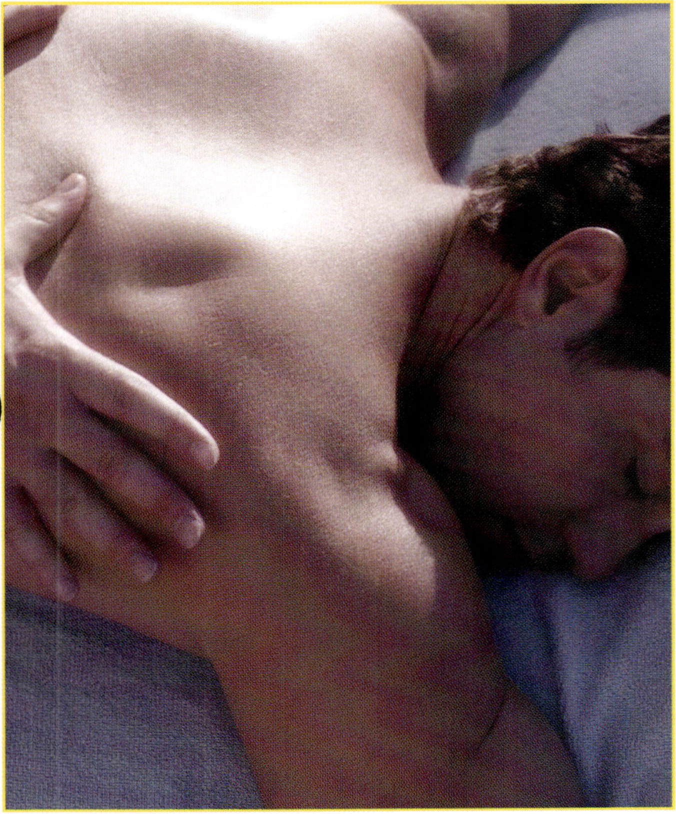

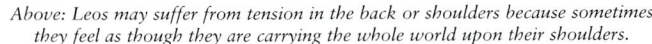

Above: Leos may suffer from tension in the back or shoulders because sometimes they feel as though they are carrying the whole world upon their shoulders.

Leo – the Sun Sign

YOUR RELATIONSHIPS

Leos excel in love. They love 'big', because they have big hearts. Anyone lucky enough to have a Lion as their partner will be lavished with affection and smothered in hugs. Leos love to give gifts, including the flattery that they need so much themselves. Lions need partners who gladly accept their warmth and are able to return it. They do not accept coolness and will dramatise all emotional situations.

Above: as a mate, they are a safe and long-term prospect. Indeed, out of all the Sun signs, the Leo heart is the most true and loyal.

Leo – the Sun Sign

They are not particularly sensitive to the feelings of others, in spite of their basic kindness. They are usually so wrapped up in themselves that they can be brutally frank and undiplomatic at times. However, this is never out of maliciousness. Unlike the Capricorn who seeks to rise socially through marriage, the Leo often does the opposite. Although a seeker of social status, the Lion prefers a 'subject', one to whom he is superior, as his partner. They have an enormous need to command and be loved by those they rule. During the courting process, Leos may drive their partners crazy with their showing off but, as a mate, they are a safe and long-term prospect. Indeed, out of all the Sun signs, the Leo heart is the most true and loyal.

YOUR RESOURCES

Leos are generous to a fault and will often put themselves in financial difficulty in order to help someone less well off than themselves. They are also extravagant and may indulge in gambling, not particularly because they believe they can win large sums of money but for the drama of being seen to be a big spender. Leos out shopping often come back with more presents for other people than for themselves, on account of their giving natures. They are never penny-pinching and tend to go for quality rather than bargains.

Leo – the Sun Sign

YOUR EDUCATION

In early school life the Lion is always the class clown. Leos are natural showmen, and like to show off their educational knowledge, often playing the role of teacher, thus putting themselves in the spotlight. Any subject that challenges their pride will be taken up, even if it is beyond the particular Lion's educational capability.

Certificates are like medals to Leos and they will do their utmost to progress through as many grades as possible. The main hindrance in the academic pursuits of the typical Leo is their tendency to laze around rather than revise for exams. However, they are quite capable of achieving a high academic status; indeed many headmasters are also Leos.

YOUR CAREER AND AMBITIONS

Any career that puts the Leo in the spotlight is the right one. Whether it is running a reception in a hotel, or actually being on stage as a performer, whatever work they choose, they make it into a performance and they are good at it. They like to be their own bosses and may at times act as if they are in charge even if they are not. They need constant reward and promotion. If they do not receive these then they lose interest in the job and leave. If they find a job where they are fully appreciated then the Leo

makes the most loyal and
faithful employee. Leos also
like to work in surroundings
befitting of royalty.

Lions make good teachers,
salespeople, lawyers and
presenters.

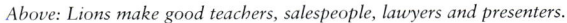

Above: Lions make good teachers, salespeople, lawyers and presenters.

Leo – the Sun Sign

YOUR FRIENDS

The Lion makes a warm and affectionate friend. Their boundless optimism means they look for the best in everybody. They express their approval openly and generously and are given to boasting about having friends in high places. However, they do have a tendency to boss their friends around and tell them what they should be doing. Once a Leo has become your friend then they are loyal and faithful and love to give their friends little gifts. Many people are attracted to Lions because they are like rays of sunshine and strive to bring happiness wherever they go.

Above: The Lion makes a warm and affectionate friend. Their boundless optimism means they look for the best in everybody.

Leo – the Sun Sign

YOUR HOPES AND FEARS

Although the Lion is big-hearted he is also extremely vulnerable. His greatest fear is loss of pride and public ridicule or humiliation, all of which can have a devastating effect on the Lion's fragile ego. Leos dislike poverty as this limits their ability to lavish gifts on their friends and family.

Above: the Lion's greatest fear is loss of pride and public ridicule or humiliation, all of which can have a devastating effect on his fragile ego.

THE TWELVE
MOON SIGNS

To find out your moon sign, either consult a professional astrologer or go to my website at www.jamespetulengro.co.uk for a free birth chart.

ARIES

An Aries Moon means that you are extremely assertive in your nature, on a subconscious level. Through the influence of Mars, life to you is one big adventure, with your ego ruling your feelings. You may come across as rather pushy because of your continual drive for success and strong self-motivation.

With your fast array of senses, you are very open to new ideas and concepts and can make quick decisions based on your instincts. It is rare that you use reasoning skills, preferring instead to leap into action. You often lose your temper over the smallest thing without a thought for the consequences. What you are thinking, you say out loud, as

your mind is always active and your emotions explode out of you, often before a proper plan can be made.

You are a bit of a rogue at times, with a *joie de vivre* which attracts many people to you. You are emotionally independent and will develop detachment from the people around you except, perhaps, from your immediate loved ones, whom you will put on a pedestal until they fall. You tend to 'feel' with your ego.

Advice is something that you rarely take, preferring instead to rely on your own instincts. If someone gives you advice when it is not asked for you can fly off the handle very quickly. The Moon in Aries may hide a sense of insecurity behind your independent and assertive exterior. You love challenges, particularly from a worthy opponent, but tend to react emotionally when you lose. You rarely compromise, particularly when it comes to your feelings. However, when it comes to romance someone who is prepared to stand up to you will earn your respect.

At home, you have a great enthusiasm for DIY but you need to be in control of both design and the work. This can often lead to domestic disputes.

The Twelve Moon Signs

TAURUS

A Taurus Moon means that you place great emphasis on material possessions. Your emotions are focused on getting the best that life has to offer. In terms of comfort, you cannot go without all of life's luxuries. You enjoy making your home environment beautiful and tasteful.

You have a great love of collecting things, including people and you can be extremely possessive about your friends and lovers. Emotionally you are very down-to-earth and practical and spend your time working to achieve your material desires in order to lead the good life that you feel you deserve. You have a natural business sense and can be very successful in the world of finance. The Moon is very stable in this sign as your emotional responses are slow but well thought out.

The Twelve Moon Signs

As a friend you are good natured, loyal and easygoing. You rarely lose your temper but when you do you can be very formidable. You would rather love than fight and can be very surprised at other people's rages. Small grievances rarely bother you. You have strong physical appetites and a deep emotional need to gratify them. You are very determined but sometimes stubborn and self-indulgent, particularly when it comes to the good things in life.

You are an affectionate and sensual lover, highly sexed too, but you have a tendency to be over-possessive as you have a strong sense of ownership in relation to both things and people. Your voice is pleasantly harmonious to others and you may well love singing and dancing and the arts in general, because Taurus is ruled by Venus, the goddess of beauty.

You are generally very conservative in your outlook and once you have decided what is true about life you will stick to it and find change of any kind difficult. You must avoid becoming too narrow-minded in your opinions.

GEMINI

A Gemini Moon makes you witty and articulate with a tendency to feel with your mind. You are adaptable in your ideas and very attracted to mental stimulation. You enjoy socialising and the sign of the twins gives you a happy and easygoing personality. Your trademark is observation and you have a great gift for verbalising all of your ideas. You are friendly and gregarious and will have many friends, lovers and acquaintances. You truly love people of all kinds. Being ruled by Mercury, the messenger god, it is likely that communication is your whole life. You are never at a loss for words but sometimes you can get carried away and end up arguing with yourself, both within your mind and within conversations and debates. This can sometimes confuse people as to what you really believe, because you can change your mind as quickly as you can change your clothes. In fact, you are likely to do both several times during a day.

The Twelve Moon Signs

Your moods can be very changeable, up one moment and down the next and you tend to be nervous in your movements. Some people may think you are shallow but actually you are torn apart by constantly changing feelings.

Your restless nature is always searching for new stimuli. Although you may not do too well academically, you are a life-long student of knowledge itself and, like a butterfly, your mind will flit from subject to subject, taking sustenance from each.

You have a great sense of humour and will be very entertaining at parties, although sometimes you can seem too cynical for some people and you can often hurt people with cutting remarks which you will forget as quickly as you have said them.

You are romantically inclined but in an intellectual way. You are fascinated more with the minds of your lovers than their bodies. You are not the most faithful of the signs as you are always looking for something or someone better around the next corner. You are not the domestic type as you are moving around too much to settle down until, perhaps, much later in life. You do not like to be tied down to one person or one place; freedom is important to you and you hate to feel restricted by emotional attachments.

CANCER

A Cancer Moon is highly sensitive, due to the fact that it is ruled by the Moon. Therefore, you can be moody and broody and your moods will fluctuate through the month, as the Moon changes from New to Full.

You are highly maternal and will mother all your friends and family if they will let you. You need to be careful not to smother them. You also have a deep and powerful capacity to memorise every experience and to re-experience it in great detail whenever you want. You also have a strong intuition and an almost psychic ability to tune in to other people's thoughts and emotions and to the atmosphere of places. You should trust in your gut feelings and hunches but because you are by nature suspicious and distrusting, you must be careful that this does not turn into paranoia. Whatever you feel, always

The Twelve Moon Signs

remember that the Moon is affecting it. You go through cycles of feelings more than any other sign. You must be careful not to mistake your own feelings for the feelings of the people around you that you are picking up on.

You are gentle, peaceful and romantic, and appreciative of all that is feminine in life. You have a great love of home and family, which you will protect with your life. Of all the signs you are the greatest home-maker. Your domestic life needs to be safe and secure as this is the shell into which the crab that you are will retreat when disturbed. Some people only see as far as your hard outer shell and forget that inside you are soft and kind.

You are particularly interested in history and your ancestors and Cancer Moons love their country. You need to feel that you are in control of the whole world and can become withdrawn and ill when you lose control of any part of it. Change is not something that you relish.

Above: you have a great love of home and family, which you will protect with your life. Of all the signs you are the greatest home-maker.

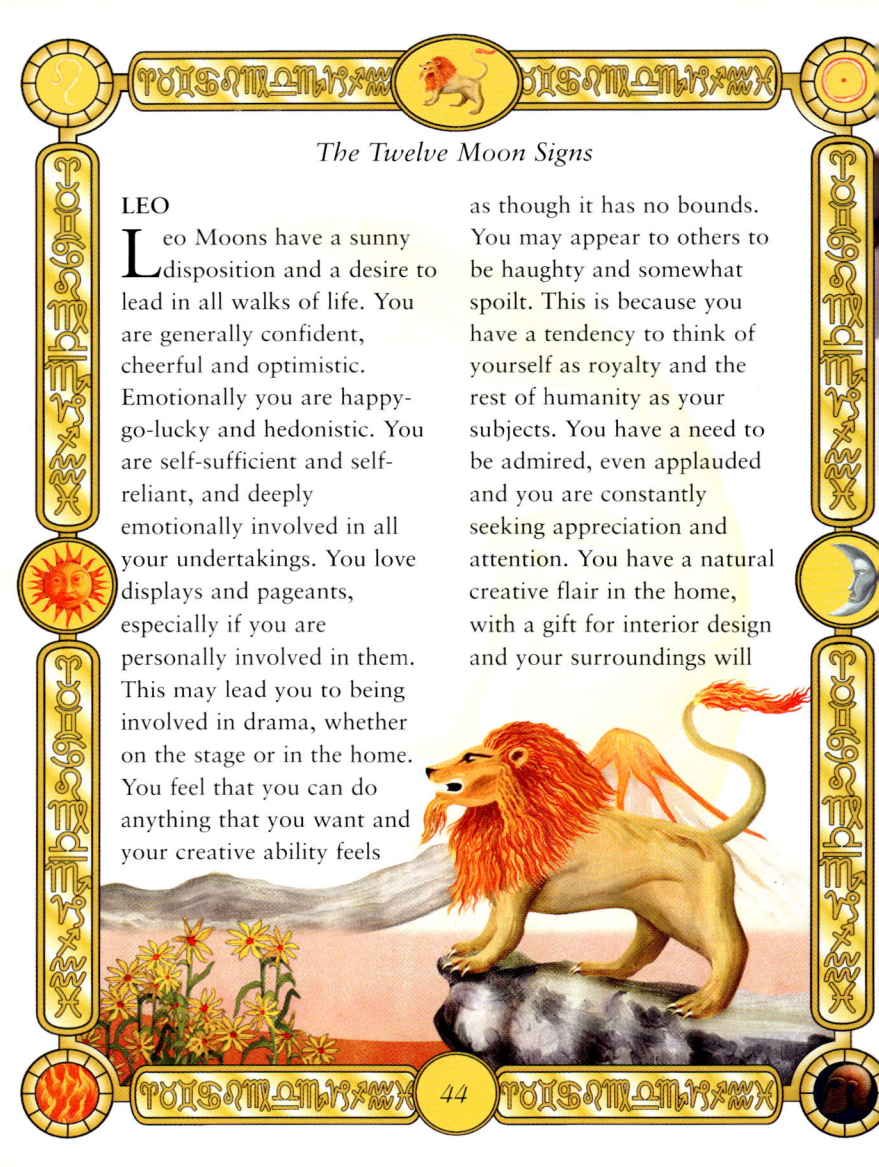

LEO

Leo Moons have a sunny disposition and a desire to lead in all walks of life. You are generally confident, cheerful and optimistic. Emotionally you are happy-go-lucky and hedonistic. You are self-sufficient and self-reliant, and deeply emotionally involved in all your undertakings. You love displays and pageants, especially if you are personally involved in them. This may lead you to being involved in drama, whether on the stage or in the home. You feel that you can do anything that you want and your creative ability feels as though it has no bounds. You may appear to others to be haughty and somewhat spoilt. This is because you have a tendency to think of yourself as royalty and the rest of humanity as your subjects. You have a need to be admired, even applauded and you are constantly seeking appreciation and attention. You have a natural creative flair in the home, with a gift for interior design and your surroundings will

The Twelve Moon Signs

straightforward and usually dignified, enabling you to gain responsibility and status.

Nothing hurts you more than when you feel unappreciated or when your pride has been stepped upon. You have a natural nobility but you can be egocentric – even pompous. You find it very difficult to back down or accept any compromise; after all, you are the Ruler. You are a loving and devoted parent and will cosset and play with your children with great affection and warmth. You love giving and have a great sense of charity towards anyone in a lesser walk of life than you. You are highly emotional with a strong drive for power and prominence.

always be flamboyant and probably expensive. You think of your home as your palace and, in seeking to impress others, you may well overspend at times.

You are a social climber and demand respect from all those around you. You are

Above: you are a social climber and demand respect from all those around you.

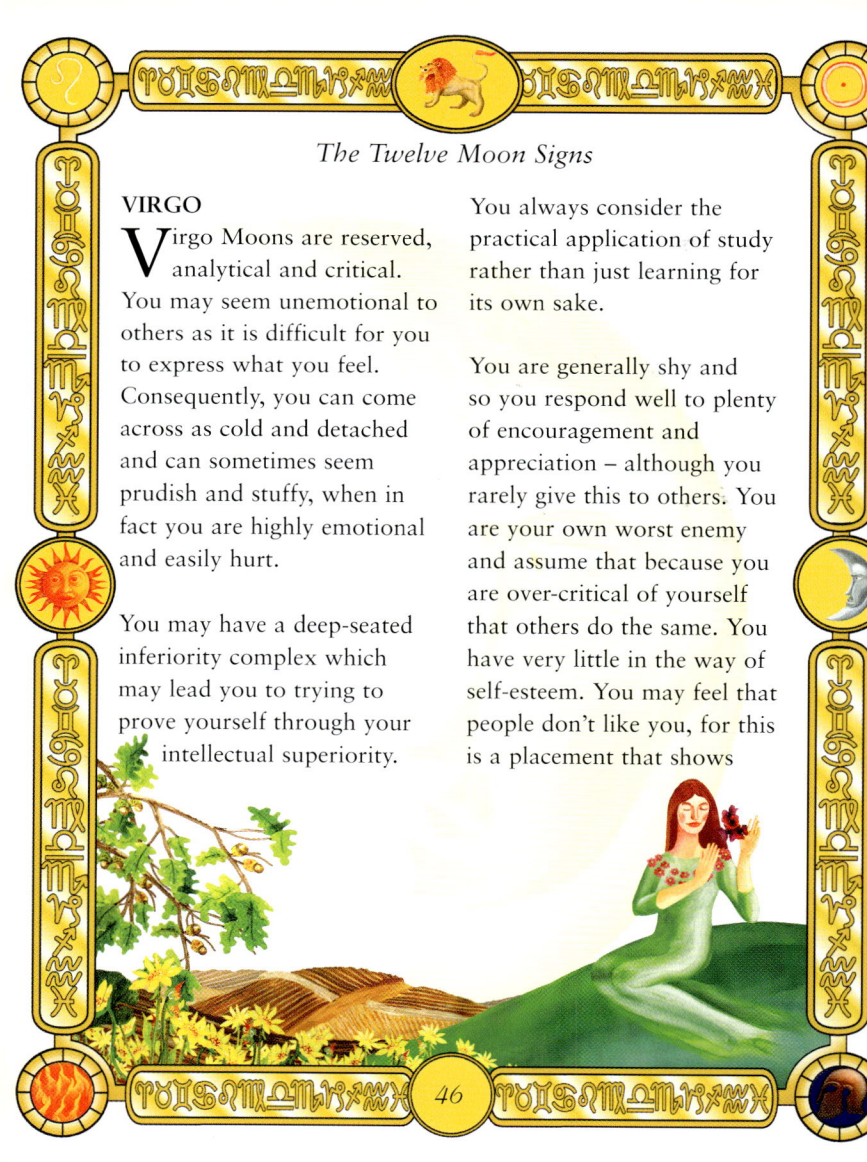

VIRGO

Virgo Moons are reserved, analytical and critical. You may seem unemotional to others as it is difficult for you to express what you feel. Consequently, you can come across as cold and detached and can sometimes seem prudish and stuffy, when in fact you are highly emotional and easily hurt.

You may have a deep-seated inferiority complex which may lead you to trying to prove yourself through your intellectual superiority.

You always consider the practical application of study rather than just learning for its own sake.

You are generally shy and so you respond well to plenty of encouragement and appreciation – although you rarely give this to others. You are your own worst enemy and assume that because you are over-critical of yourself that others do the same. You have very little in the way of self-esteem. You may feel that people don't like you, for this is a placement that shows

The Twelve Moon Signs

much lack of self-esteem, thus you tend to be emotionally reserved. Your talents lie in expressing your feelings through writing and poetry because your Moon is ruled by Mercury, the messenger god. Consequently you will be ruled by your mind rather than by your heart and you will have trouble understanding highly emotional and passionate people. Your reactions often seem detached and rather cold. Self-analysis may occupy a lot of your thoughts and in fact psychoanalysis or psychiatry would be good careers for you.

You are too introverted to have a strong sex drive and you will be shy about the physical act and have difficulty in accepting its

undignified side. Within a relationship you will attempt to make yourself indispensable to your partner, thereby securing their love. You respond well to responsibility. In the home you are particularly concerned with hygiene, health and diet and will be constantly involved in tidying up and cleaning.

Virgo Moon is an earthy moon, so you are practical and have a definite sense of the realities of life. You are at your best when you are taking care of someone who is in need of you. You can be temperamental and argumentative but you have a shrewd business sense and always pay meticulous attention to detail.

LIBRA

Libra Moons are gentle, tolerant and have a great sense of beauty and justice. You are, above all things, dependent upon your personal relationships. The symbol of Libra, the scales, signifies balance and symmetry in all things. You are diplomatic, broad-minded, sociable and make pleasant company. You dislike disorder and spend a great deal of your time organising your busy social life. You are even-tempered, well mannered and graceful in movement. As you are ruled by Venus, art and beauty are paramount in your life, as is your search for the perfect partner. You hate coarseness or vulgarity and will seek to have relationships with cultured and educated people. You are highly adaptable and dislike disputes, conflicts and disorder. Your gentle nature will bring you many friends but because of your tendency to weigh things in the balance, you may never be sure of how you feel about people. You can find it hard to make up your mind quickly and will spend a great deal of time considering the various possibilities and options open to you in all areas of your life.

The Twelve Moon Signs

Your home, which is very important to you, will be harmonious and tranquil and full of beautiful objects. You are particularly attracted towards the arts and may make a career in this direction. Anything that you can make more beautiful will be given a makeover, including people.

You enjoy the company of people and do not like to spend much time alone. You need to be liked and your emotional wellbeing depends on being appreciated for the beautiful person that you really are, for you truly are a thoughtful and good-natured person who will go out of their way to be kind to others. At many times in your life you will seem to be in crisis and have difficulty in making decisions because you are capable of seeing both sides equally. As often as not your decision will be based on the toss of a coin. You are sometimes too willing to compromise and frequently you allow others to take advantage of you in the cause of peace – possibly because you find it easier to let other people make the decisions. For your partner you can be self-sacrificial and happy to fulfil his or her needs above your own.

A solid, steady relationship is your preference. You love to receive small gifts and you are a romantic at heart, doing your best to spread beauty and harmony wherever you can.

SCORPIO

Scorpio Moons are the most passionate and secretive of all the signs. You are highly sensitive and have an uncanny memory which leads you to remember both pleasant and unpleasant memories – which can sometimes leave deep psychic scars. You enjoy life to the full and have an innate understanding that through suffering, character is formed. You are the most sexual of all the signs but you combine your sexuality with deep spirituality. Pluto, ruler of the underworld, can lead you into the depths of your unconscious where you may find disturbing feelings but, having entered into that Underworld, you are likely to return strangely refreshed and born anew.

You have a great capacity for regeneration and will 'die' many times during your lifetime. Change is what you thrive on. You must learn to come to terms with your deep emotions as other signs are not as emotionally intense as you. You may find that

The Twelve Moon Signs

you view other people as shallow. Your real nature is not openly apparent to others because until you get to know somebody deeply, you tend to hide your true feelings. However, once you love you love passionately, and the object of your affection can take over your whole existence. This can also be so with regard to your children, as you will bestow an all-consuming love upon them. You are a good homemaker, providing that you get your own way in it, but you much prefer the company of your immediate family to entertaining all and sundry. In all your relationships you are extremely possessive and jealous and can even become violent when your passions

are thwarted. No-one says 'No' to a Scorpio Moon. You can be domineering and will often use sexual favours to get what you want. You have a problem with judging people too quickly and, if they make a mistake, you rarely give them a second chance. You react to emotional situations in an abrupt and impulsive way. You can also be vindictive, spiteful and vengeful when wronged and are easily hurt.

You are very determined in achieving your ambitions and thrive on new challenges. You are an extremist in nature and never pursue anything light-heartedly. Even when a situation becomes detrimental to your nature, you insist on seeing it through to the end.

SAGITTARIUS

A Sagittarius Moon gives feelings of restlessness and requires a great deal of physical activity in order to disperse pent-up emotion. You need your freedom to wander where and when you will. You are happy-go-lucky, enthusiastic, highly optimistic and at your best when you are mobile. Because of your eternal optimism you can be socially naïve and blissfully unaware of social differences. This naïvety can sometimes make you socially inept because you tend to see all people as equals.

You have high ideals and meet people on your own terms by melting and merging into relationships with them as a friendly puppy does. You are generally good natured, fun loving and jovial – like the planet Jupiter that rules this sign. You always know who you are and where you are heading but are adaptable enough to change direction when it feels that you'll learn more by doing so. Learning is very important to you, although you have a tendency not to learn from your mistakes. The learning that you are interested in is the knowledge of all things, particularly the mysteries of the universe. You make a fine teacher or spiritual adviser.

Your home may not be tidy but will be filled with objects you have gathered on your travels. You will be very enthusiastic in teaching your children everything they want to know, encouraging them whenever you can to expand their knowledge, behaving more as a friend than parent.

It is important to you that your partners are also your friends as well as your lovers. You display your affections openly and need a partner who will play, socialise and travel to places with you without making too many demands. Being free and without restraints is one of your deepest needs.

As you have a predisposition to overindulge in eating and drinking, sporting activities are a great help in keeping your weight down. You are prone to many changes in your life, particularly those relating to your residence or career – these are changes which you need to bring about in order to fulfil your restless nature.

CAPRICORN

Capricorn Moons want to be recognised as important and powerful people because they were raised that way. You were likely to have had a strong parental influence. You are determined, steadfast and reliable. You are geared up to lead and have a strong sense of politics. You are the most ambitious of all the signs and the most likely to succeed in your emotional arena.

You seek power and are continually 'climbing mountains'. Once you have reached the top of your particular mountain it is almost guaranteed that you will notice a higher mountain in the distance for you to climb – and off you will go again.

It can sometimes be difficult for you to express your emotions and some people may see you as unfeeling but you are not. Your emotions are aimed at your career and it is hard for you to relax, let go and enjoy life's simple pleasures. You are the parent of the Zodiac because of the rulership of Saturn, the god of

The Twelve Moon Signs

time. Due to this, you are likely to seem old when you are young and young when you are old. Some Moon in Capricorns have a Peter Pan complex but only inside; on the outside they often appear to be wise beyond their years. Whatever your goals, you will strive to achieve them, stubbornly and persistently. You are a very hard worker and will take on goals that would frighten other signs.

You are conservative in your emotions, not in the political sense, but in the true sense of conservation. This is your way, not to create new things but to improve upon and conserve what has come

before you. If you are thwarted in your goals you can become despondent and moody, and begin to look at the negative side of things. You need to develop a more optimistic approach to life. Capricorn Moons can be shy but they have a very clever sense of humour and can lead people to do what they want by using this humour.

Your home life, like your career, will be ambitious. You will want to live in the best house in the best part of town. A Capricorn Moon loves renovating old property and your taste is normally classical. A lot of Capricorn Moons work from home, due

The Twelve Moon Signs

to their tendency to be shy and self-conscious about their feelings – feelings which they would really rather not have. With your children you are likely to be a disciplinarian and have as much ambition for them as you have yourself. Sometimes you can be disappointed because they don't have the same drive and it can be hard for you to show your real, deep feelings of affection towards them. You may aspire to being a

member of the aristocracy and you are most certainly a social climber, although you would prefer to entertain at home than to go to parties. It is rare to find a Capricorn Moon who leaves the world poorer than he or she entered it. You are the most reserved of signs, particularly in the way you communicate and interact with others. Your driving ambitions are usually successful but they are sometimes at the expense of your romantic life.

Security and stability are very important to you, as are financial gain and the need to establish yourself as a leader of the community. You are a traditionalist in life and have solid values and morals.

The Twelve Moon Signs

AQUARIUS

Aquarius Moons produce the most modern and progressive people of all the signs. However, you can sometimes be erratic in some of the ideals you hold. You are unusual, unpredictable, and have a big imagination. You are most likely to engage in many kinds of group activities and have a wide range of friends from all walks of life. You have a capacity to see inside people and not be taken in by surfaces. For you a beggar may be an angel in disguise.

You have a very creative imagination and your many friends will value your input into their lives. Sometimes your high ideals can get in the way of practicality and common sense. You have a quality that puts you ahead of your time and some people may see you as downright eccentric. You are attracted to all things that are modern and innovative because you are ruled by the planet Uranus, god of change. You love the sciences and would dearly love to invent something to improve the lot of humanity.

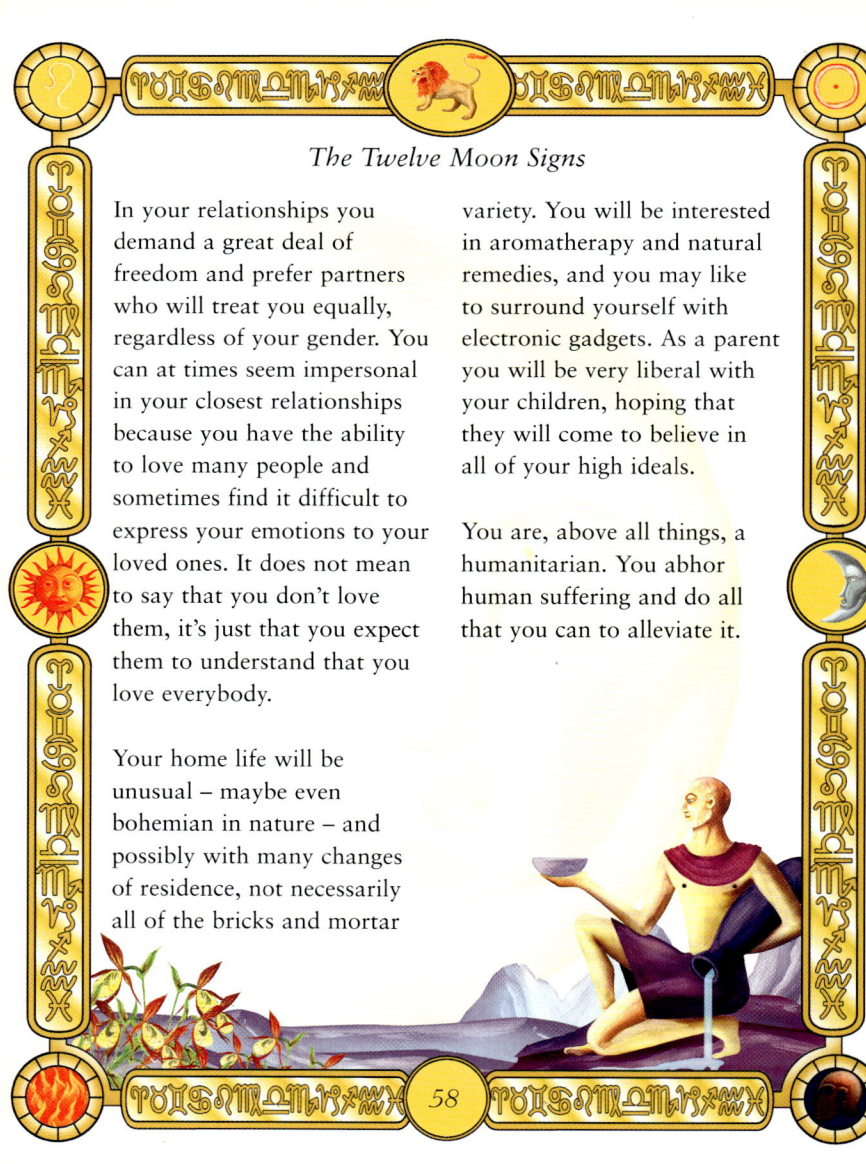

The Twelve Moon Signs

In your relationships you demand a great deal of freedom and prefer partners who will treat you equally, regardless of your gender. You can at times seem impersonal in your closest relationships because you have the ability to love many people and sometimes find it difficult to express your emotions to your loved ones. It does not mean to say that you don't love them, it's just that you expect them to understand that you love everybody.

Your home life will be unusual – maybe even bohemian in nature – and possibly with many changes of residence, not necessarily all of the bricks and mortar variety. You will be interested in aromatherapy and natural remedies, and you may like to surround yourself with electronic gadgets. As a parent you will be very liberal with your children, hoping that they will come to believe in all of your high ideals.

You are, above all things, a humanitarian. You abhor human suffering and do all that you can to alleviate it.

The Twelve Moon Signs

PISCES

A Moon in Pisces means that you have a great understanding of what it is to be human, albeit in a somewhat dreamy sense. You are blessed with sensitivity and perception, allowing you to show great compassion and consideration for other people.

This Moon sign means you have great empathy towards others in a psychic way and you often experience their emotions. Since Neptune, god of the sea rules your Moon, you need to ensure that you are not psychically flooded by other people's moods and desires. You should also meditate and reflect on your own feelings in solitude.

Life to you is permanently rose-tinted, no matter how harsh the reality. Everyone's 'little faults' are ignored, no matter how big. At times, though, your over-optimism and unselfishness can leave you open to others taking advantage of your passive nature. Your misplaced trust means that you often end up hurt and feeling sorry for yourself. Rather than blame the other person, you tend to turn on yourself, which again results in melancholy.

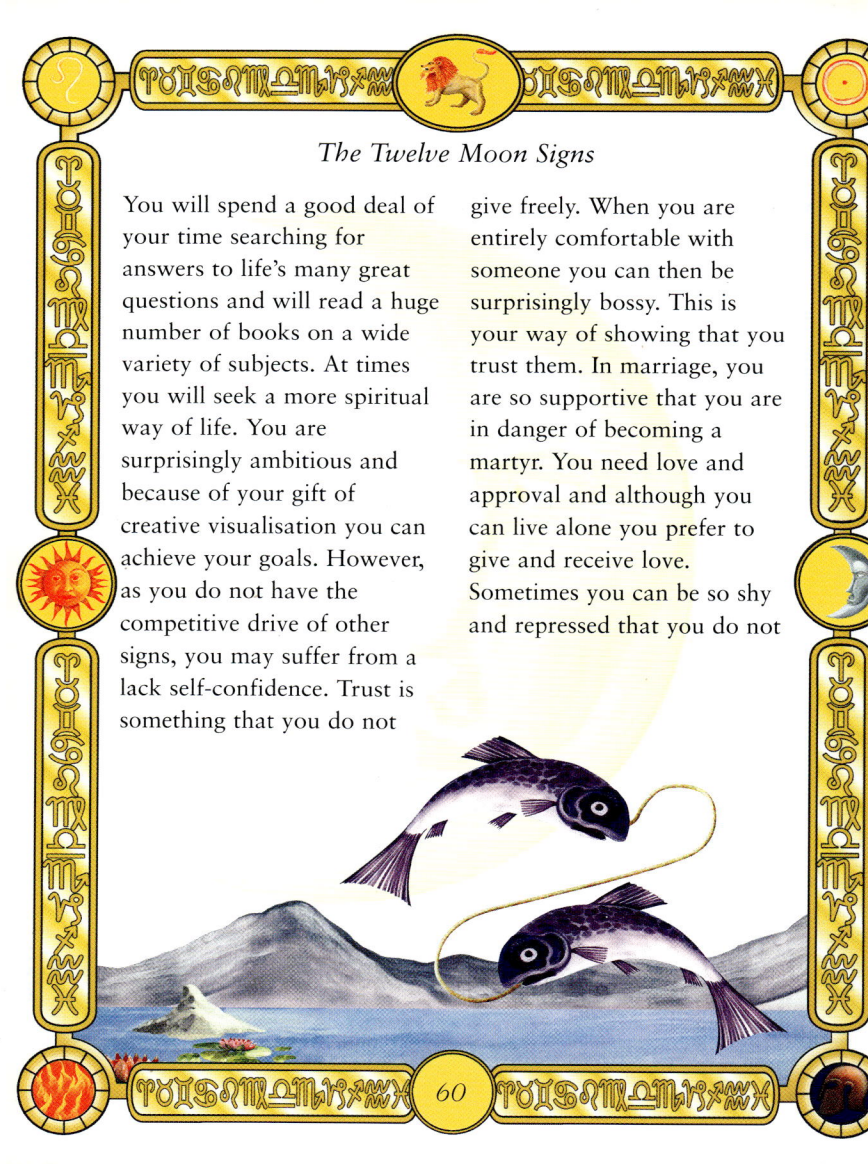

The Twelve Moon Signs

You will spend a good deal of your time searching for answers to life's many great questions and will read a huge number of books on a wide variety of subjects. At times you will seek a more spiritual way of life. You are surprisingly ambitious and because of your gift of creative visualisation you can achieve your goals. However, as you do not have the competitive drive of other signs, you may suffer from a lack self-confidence. Trust is something that you do not give freely. When you are entirely comfortable with someone you can then be surprisingly bossy. This is your way of showing that you trust them. In marriage, you are so supportive that you are in danger of becoming a martyr. You need love and approval and although you can live alone you prefer to give and receive love. Sometimes you can be so shy and repressed that you do not

The Twelve Moon Signs

find the love you require and retreat into yourself instead. As a parent you empathise with your children but prefer those that can actively respond, rather than young babies. You are incredibly romantic and love all the little things which make up a relationship. Sex is something you enjoy as it combines all your favourite feelings and sensations.

Your home is your haven, a place where you can withdraw from the hustle and bustle of everyday life. Even so, you will also have many friends and visitors coming and going, especially as you rarely lock your doors. People are drawn to you because they know you are a good shoulder to cry on and will

assist as much as possible with their personal problems. You need to ensure, however, that you do not sacrifice yourself for others too much.

Above: people are drawn to you because they know you are a good shoulder to cry on.

LEO SUN

AND THE TWELVE MOON SIGN COMBINATIONS

When you calculate a birth chart, you will discover that the Moon as well as other planets will sometimes be in different signs of the Zodiac. The whole chart gives the entire picture of the personality but the Sun and the Moon have the most powerful effect upon us. When you combine the Sun sign and the Moon sign you are combining different parts of the Zodiac. Some signs work well together and some signs do not; in the same way that two Sun signs may live in eternal conflict where others live in harmony, so it is with the Sun and Moon in your chart. What follows is an explanation of the combinations between your Leo Sun and various other moons that may appear in your birth chart.

LEO SUN WITH ARIES MOON

The double fire combination of your Sun and Moon signs produces a personality with a strong drive and emotional intensity. Because you have no fear, you display great courage and are always looking for challenges and obstacles to overcome. Whatever you do, you throw yourself into it with total commitment. Unfortunately you do have a quick temper and when you roar you really roar. When your honour is questioned, even to the slightest degree, your defence mechanism invariably goes into overdrive and you may bite people's heads off. You enjoy a good battle and attack every problem as if it were going to attack you. You usually manage to pre-empt any unpleasant situation which may arise.

You will pursue any possibility to enhance your self-confident image and whatever you do go after, you go at with great relish and fervour. You are rash and impulsive and willing to try out any idea that comes

along. You never hesitate to assume responsibilities or meet obligations. Although you always appear to be in complete control, inwardly you do not consider yourself to be particularly clever, although you will never show this weakness. You do need to be careful that you do not seek to dominate everyone around you. If you are able to stop your ego from always being centre stage, then you will be very successful.

LEO SUN WITH TAURUS MOON

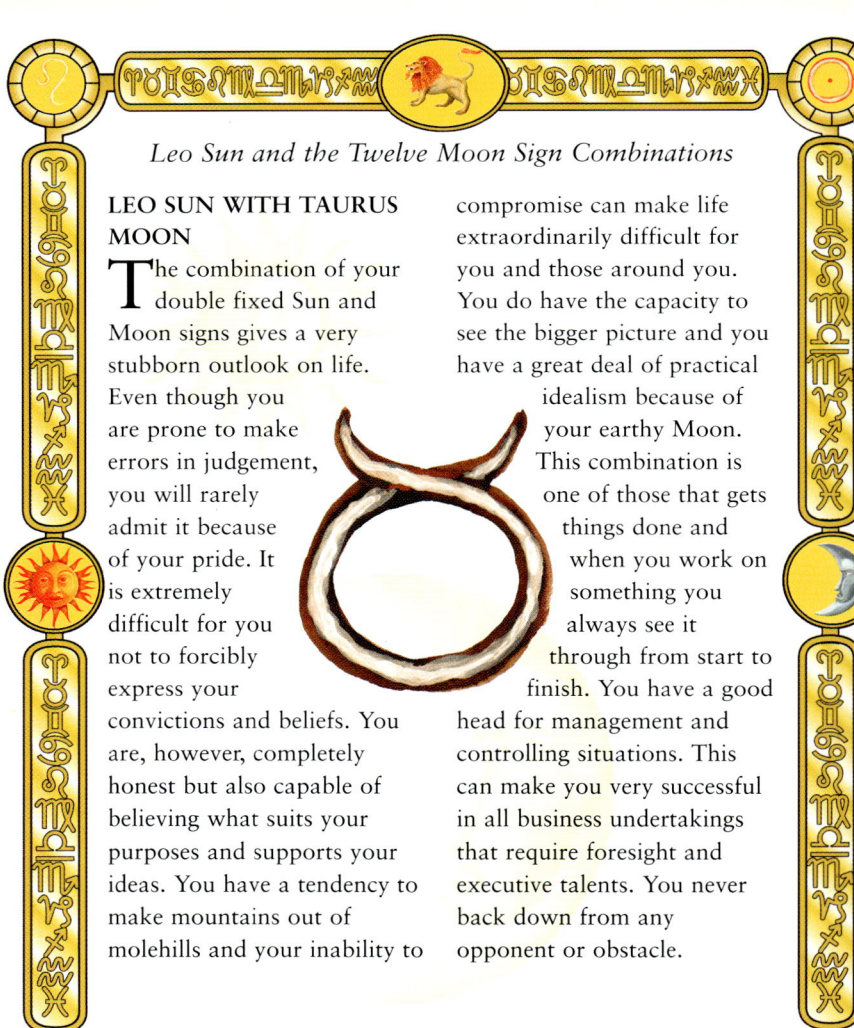

The combination of your double fixed Sun and Moon signs gives a very stubborn outlook on life. Even though you are prone to make errors in judgement, you will rarely admit it because of your pride. It is extremely difficult for you not to forcibly express your convictions and beliefs. You are, however, completely honest but also capable of believing what suits your purposes and supports your ideas. You have a tendency to make mountains out of molehills and your inability to compromise can make life extraordinarily difficult for you and those around you. You do have the capacity to see the bigger picture and you have a great deal of practical idealism because of your earthy Moon. This combination is one of those that gets things done and when you work on something you always see it through from start to finish. You have a good head for management and controlling situations. This can make you very successful in all business undertakings that require foresight and executive talents. You never back down from any opponent or obstacle.

You are also very loving and giving with those who are close to you but you demand their complete devotion, admiration and constant love. You are a well-meaning and sincere person but you need to learn to become a little more detached so that you are able to see yourself a bit more objectively. You have a very traditional outlook on life and a great reverence for your family, for whom you would readily give your life.

LEO SUN WITH GEMINI MOON

The combination of your fiery Sun and airy Moon means that you are a person who can put all your ideas into action. You have the vitality, generosity, warmth and strength of Leo balanced with the mental adaptability of Gemini. You are always looking for ways to impress others through your achievements, particularly your intellectual ones. You are intuitive about people and are able to make a good impression on them by knowing what they want. Your ideas, although not based on deep philosophical

constructs, are always plausible and always delivered in a persuasive manner. You are best working in a career that allows your mind to flow and will never need to work hard for a living. You tend to look for easy money and always know the best way to go about getting it, without expending a lot of physical energy. Although you may be considered physically lazy, your mind is constantly alert and looking for openings. However, this high level of sustained mental activity can sometimes turn you into a bundle of nerves.

You are always trying to impress everyone with what you know – and you do know a lot. Therefore, you make an extremely interesting conversationalist and dinner party guest. You love to entertain and have a knack of gathering guests who are also stimulating and interesting. Your sharp observations make you very popular in those social circles. Your character is particularly suited to working within the media, public relations or advertising.

LEO SUN WITH CANCER MOON

The combination of your Sun sign and Moon sign, with both planets in their own signs, results in a well balanced personality. You have a sunny disposition on the outside and this is also reflected within your Leo Sun's positivity, which reduces the Cancerian tendency towards moodiness and negativity. Equally, the Leo's normal tendency to seek the spotlight is balanced and controlled by the modesty of your quieter Cancer Moon. You make a sympathetic friend and an understanding listener, which attracts many people to you. You enjoy stimulating company and your friends will confide in you because you are dependable and trustworthy. Your big heart allows you to help people when there is a need, often acting as a mother figure. You have a high sense of self-worth, so you have no need to try and impress others with your achievements.

You are realistic and have a great deal of common sense. Your feet are planted firmly on the ground. Romance and love are very important to you but you will never be happy until you find someone

Leo Sun and the Twelve Moon Sign Combinations

upon whom you can lavish your affections. You have a very sound character, great persistence and honest desire to be a good person. Your home is where you centre your creative energies. You believe strongly in traditional family values and, accordingly, your family life will be warm and stable.

LEO SUN WITH LEO MOON

You were born around the time of the New Moon and this double combination of your Sun sign and Moon sign results in a forceful and

Above: your home is where you centre your creative energies. You believe strongly in traditional family values.

Leo Sun and the Twelve Moon Sign Combinations

ambitious personality that wants to achieve a great deal of success in their life. You have a driving ambition to rule your world. On the surface you appear jovial and sunny but underneath, there is a ruthless streak in you that never forgets or forgives any injury to your pride or vanity. You are authoritative and look for leadership and prominence in life but you will pursue this with your normally happy and friendly personality. You have a tremendous amount of self-control but, emotionally, you have a need to be worshiped. As a result of this need, you respond to flattery more than any other sign.

You have a tendency to be excessive in your approach to life, even in your negative emotions. When you are aroused you go all the way, and can be extremely destructive towards anyone that gets in your way. However, you hold no malice and remain detached and impersonal. You have a very strong will but are a bit too self-centred at times. You have a need to dazzle others with your magnificence and have no time for details because for you, the broader picture is enough. You will probably be drawn to drama and, if you are, your dramatic skills will need to be drawn to the heights as you will never be happy in a subordinate role. You have the stuff that stars are made out of.

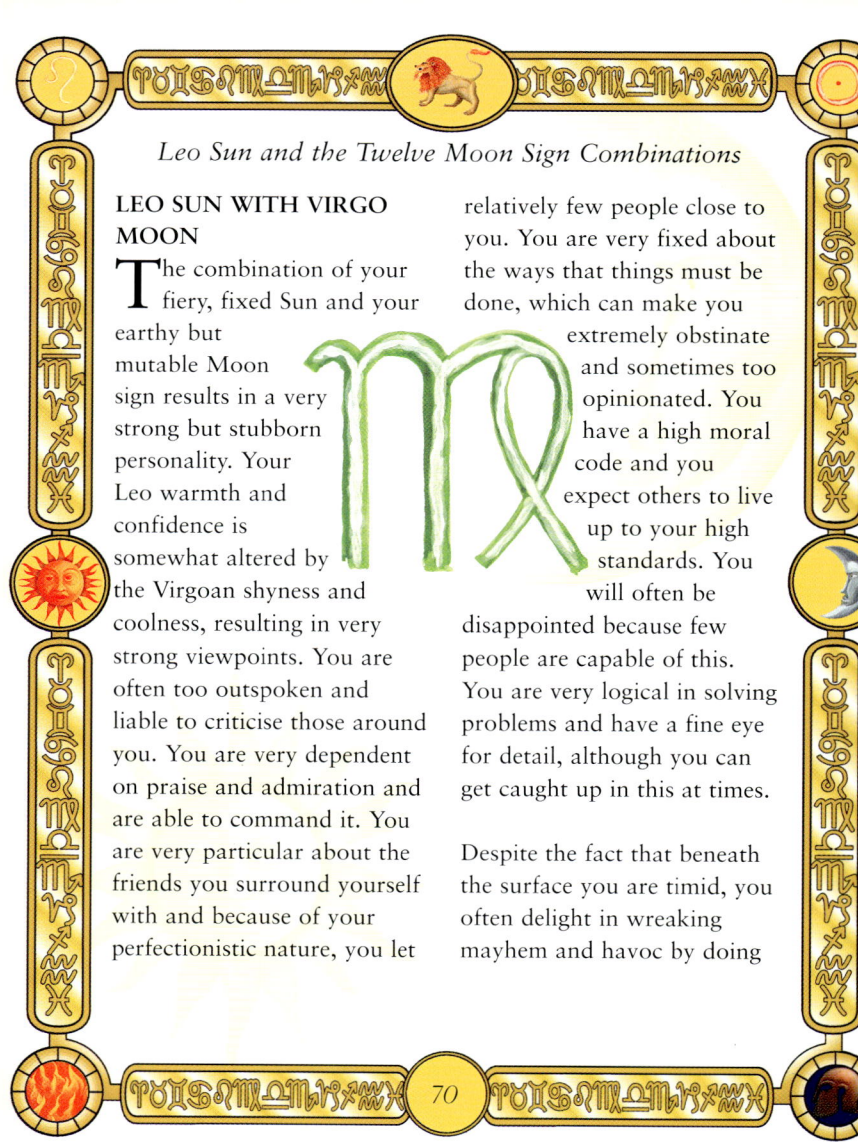

LEO SUN WITH VIRGO MOON

The combination of your fiery, fixed Sun and your earthy but mutable Moon sign results in a very strong but stubborn personality. Your Leo warmth and confidence is somewhat altered by the Virgoan shyness and coolness, resulting in very strong viewpoints. You are often too outspoken and liable to criticise those around you. You are very dependent on praise and admiration and are able to command it. You are very particular about the friends you surround yourself with and because of your perfectionistic nature, you let relatively few people close to you. You are very fixed about the ways that things must be done, which can make you extremely obstinate and sometimes too opinionated. You have a high moral code and you expect others to live up to your high standards. You will often be disappointed because few people are capable of this. You are very logical in solving problems and have a fine eye for detail, although you can get caught up in this at times.

Despite the fact that beneath the surface you are timid, you often delight in wreaking mayhem and havoc by doing the opposite of what is the norm for you. Because other people do not realise that you are just play-acting when you are being mischievous, you can seem callous. Your dry sense of humour is rarely understood by 'lesser mortals'. Normally you are charming and polite, which can help you to be successful but you need to be careful of your over-critical nature and your sharp tongue. You do not suffer fools gladly and you make sure they know it. You need to learn tact and diplomacy but you are always scrupulously honest and basically kind-hearted.

LEO SUN WITH LIBRA MOON

The combination of your fiery Sun and your Moon sign ruled by Venus, the planet of beauty, makes you a passionate and romantic person with a warm-hearted and sentimental approach to life.

You are conventional and traditional, with a healthy respect for public opinion. You are also tolerant, open-minded, honourable and loyal. However, you rarely reveal your true nature to others, doing so only after they prove their loyalty. This can make you seem elusive and hard to pin down.

Leo Sun and the Twelve Moon Sign Combinations

You take time before you commit yourself to any action but you have an instinctive understanding of what people want from you. Your opinions are usually well thought out and based on solid foundations, which earns you a great deal of respect. On account of your capacity for clear thinking, you are not a person of extremes. You are also highly blessed with the gifts of a strong imagination and creative talent. Because there is much that is dramatic in your makeup, you are most likely to work within the arts and drama.

Although you are able to live independently, you need to find more depth to your emotions, particularly in your relationships. You can be over-cautious about getting too romantically involved and some people could regard you as frivolous. Other people's emotions will often make you retreat into yourself. This is because you are a keen observer of human nature and notice that strong emotions often lead to hurt. Once you do settle on a partner, you will be very affectionate and highly sensual towards them. You have a great sense of style, both in your appearance and surroundings. You also have a good head for business matters but you can easily become too accustomed to having things your own way.

Leo Sun and the Twelve Moon Sign Combinations

LEO SUN WITH SCORPIO MOON

This combination of your fiery Sun combined with your Pluto-ruled Moon produces a highly passionate and emotional personality. This is a very powerful and dynamic mixture; at times you are like a volcano waiting to erupt and when you do, you pour forth and vent your feelings. You are extremely temperamental at times and need to learn to keep control over your inner rage and direct your energies to more constructive outcomes. Both your signs are fixed in nature, therefore your opinions and likes and dislikes are unshakeable. You are not one to be swayed by any logical argument about what you believe in and, regardless of what it is, you are certain you are right. The negative side of this can make you bigoted but the positive side is that your instincts are often right. These strong instincts, plus your natural alertness, makes you quick to pick up on any problems before they have had the chance to start.

Although you have high moral standards, you are often unable to meet them as your passion often takes over from your reason. You also have a tendency to judge others by these high standards and can find many people wanting. Other less dynamic signs can irritate you with

Leo Sun and the Twelve Moon Sign Combinations

their perceived slowness. You see yourself at centre stage and sometimes ignore the emotional needs of others. You must curb your tendency to over-dramatise situations and learn to become less possessive and self-centred. This lack of objectivity does mean that you can act upon ideas very quickly, though.

Your natural magnetism and attractiveness can give you great success as a leader in any walk of life you choose. You are extremely capable and determined, and have a great deal of pride and confidence in your self. Friends and colleagues will respect you, both for your honesty and your capacity for hard work. At times, though,

you are bent on achieving power and authority and anyone who stands in the way of this is likely to feel the full force of your personality. As an opponent you are formidable and relentless in your attack but, as a friend, you are fiercely loyal and will help out, even with personal problems.

Above: you are extremely capable and determined, and have a great deal of pride and confidence in your self.

Leo Sun and the Twelve Moon Sign Combinations

LEO SUN WITH SAGITTARIUS MOON

The double fire combination of your Sun sign and Moon sign gives a restlessness and a need for constant movement. You are always looking for exciting adventures and whatever situation you find yourself in, you want to change it. After all, in your world, the grass is always greener. You are continually seeking a new game to play, whether it is a mountain to climb or a new country to visit. Your love of competitive activity gives you a need to win through, however hard the challenge might be.

You have a boundless imagination and the feet to follow it. It is hard for you to settle down to one job, one place or one partner because of this. You sometimes get into trouble by being too honest, never mincing your words or sparing the feelings of others but you are never cruel. As long as you are constantly on the move you will be happy, but whenever you feel tired or dependent you will become depressed.

The mix of Leo's vitality and warmth, with Jupiterian joviality and honesty gives you a very optimistic outlook on life. You believe that you can do anything and go anywhere and indeed, you

have the capacity to make your dreams come true. You have an enthusiastic but restless mind, always on the alert for a new project. However, sometimes you are pursuing so many different goals that you end up not achieving any of them because you burn yourself out in the effort. If you are able to channel your energies into one goal at a time and remain true to it, you will achieve your aim faster than any other sign.

LEO SUN WITH CAPRICORN MOON

The combination of your fiery Sun sign and earthy Moon sign results in a highly ambitious personality. You expect a great deal from all aspects of your life and your strong sense of purpose ensures you meet your targets with success. You are mentally alert at all times and make a formidable opponent. Indeed, you ensure that your reputation and appearance is impeccable. You always have a friendly and amicable exterior and rarely expose your inner determination and resolve. This is because you have no need to be understood. You have high self-esteem and expect others to respect you.

Leo Sun and the Twelve Moon Sign Combinations

To be successful you believe you need to build up a reputation for integrity and reliability, qualities that you have in abundance.

Your aim in life is to be seen as an authority figure who is trustworthy and impeccable. You have a very strong ambition and back this up with great willpower and strength of purpose. You may become melancholy at times when you feel that you are not achieving your goals, but you will hide your doubts from even your closest companions. You are more likely to succeed in a traditional field of work, providing that you curb your tendency to ride roughshod over your competitors.

LEO SUN WITH AQUARIUS MOON

You were born around the time of the Full Moon, when your Sun and Moon signs were in opposition. This combination results in an unusual and perhaps eccentric personality. The mixture of the generosity and pride of Leo with the originality and modern approach of Aquarius means that whatever you undertake will be met by popular support. You are highly sociable and a total extrovert. You are also very philosophical and have a natural desire to project yourself into group work, or work with the general public. You are highly idealistic and attracted to all

New Age ideas but you remain detached, never getting too involved or committed. You may drift from one school of thought to another like a butterfly, taking sustenance from the knowledge and then moving on. You are also highly romantic and will sometimes be drawn to situations that are impractical. It is unlikely for you to focus on one idea or one person for very long.

You are not very ambitious, again because of your lack of focus and commitment. You like knowing a little about everything, so you have a tendency to

change your job or career many times. Although others may see you as superficial, you know better. Your self-esteem is rarely dented and you usually thoroughly enjoy your exciting life.

LEO SUN WITH PISCES MOON

The combination of your fiery Sun and watery Moon sign results in a very kind-hearted and loveable demeanour. The two signs bring out the best in each other, resulting in a noble and confident Lion with the deep, intuitive nature of Pisces. You dream of making your loved ones and those

Leo Sun and the Twelve Moon Sign Combinations

around you as happy and secure as possible. You empathise with, and know the emotional needs of others, always having the time and patience to listen to them in order to help. You are never emotionally detached and always advise them straight from your big heart. This may sometimes cause you problems as you are continually running around for people, never able to say no to anyone who requires your assistance. You may get overwhelmed at times with the problems of others. You are an extremely deep thinker, so you need to ensure that you avoid getting depressed or too exhausted. Fortunately, you attract good friends who can keep your spirits up.

You have very high ideals and do your utmost to live by them and set an example. You have a very confident and assertive exterior, which bubbles with great enthusiasm but, inside, you are serious and sensitive and have very profound, philosophical thoughts. You are extremely open and honest and it is hard for you to fool others. However, it is rare that you are fooled in turn as your incredible intuition means you can see into the very hearts of others.

EPILOGUE

Now that you have read this book you may be wondering what use it can be to you. To understand the inner workings of your personality and emotions will allow you to realise your full potential, and astrology is a simple and effective way to achieve this. There is, of course, much more to the subject of astrology than just the Sun and Moon signs. There are all the planets to take into consideration and the houses they fall in. As I said at the beginning, every birth chart is unique, but there are similarities between us all. It is the differences that make us individuals. I hope that in the reading of this book perhaps you will be inspired to look deeper into yourself and deeper into the uses of astrology.

"Know yourself and the truth will set you free"